QUICK and EASY COOKING

Edited by Jane Solmson

WEATHERVANE BOOKS

New York
Sydney, Auckland, London, New York.

This edition is published by Weathervane Books,
    distributed by Crown Publishers, Inc.
a b c d e f g h

Published under arrangement with Ottenheimer Publishers, Inc.
Printed in the United States of America

CONTENTS

Beef Tartare

Beef Tartare

1 pound chuck, round sirloin, or tenderloin steak
Freshly ground black pepper

Buy and grind steak as near serving time as possible. Meat becomes dark in color if left standing.

Add only pepper to meat.

Shape meat into 4 equal-sized cakes. Make a depression in center of each with spoon.

4 large raw onion rings
4 raw egg yolks
4 anchovy fillets
2 teaspoons capers

Place an onion ring around this depression.

Put an egg yolk into center of each.

Sprinkle few capers on top egg yolk or serve on side.

Lay one curled anchovy fillet on top each yolk or serve on side.

Few chives
Fresh horseradish if available (optional)

Decorate with few chives or horseradish.

4 quarters lemon (optional)

Serve with rye bread and butter, or French bread and lemon quarters.

Yield: 4 servings.

Potted Herb Cheese

3 cups grated cheddar
    cheese
1 tablespoon whipping
    cream
2 tablespoons sherry
6 tablespoons butter
1 teaspoon chopped chives
1 teaspoon tarragon leaves
1 teaspoon sage
1 teaspoon thyme
1 teaspoon parsley flakes

Clarified butter

Let come to room temperature;
serve with fingers of hot
buttered toast or tiny, hot
biscuits.

Yield: 1 pint.

Place all ingredients except clarified butter in top of
    double boiler over hot water.
Stir over medium heat until cheese and butter melt and
    mixture is thoroughly blended.
Pour into pint jar; chill until cold.
Cover with ¼-inch-deep layer clarified butter.
Cover; store in refrigerator.

Potted Herb Cheese

Liver Pâté

¼ pound butter or chicken
    fat
1 large onion, chopped fine
1 pound chicken livers

1 tablespoon Worcestershire
    sauce
Salt and pepper to taste

Melt butter in medium skillet; lightly tan chopped onion.

Add chicken livers; cook until slightly pink at center, about
    5 minutes. Remove from heat.
Put entire mixture through food mill until ground very
    smooth. If you use colander instead of food mill, you
    may want to put liver mixture through twice to ensure
    smooth texture.
Add Worcestershire sauce, salt, and pepper. Mix together
    well with spoon.

Shape pâté into greased mold for a party.
Turn out on serving plate, surround with party crackers so
    guests can help themselves.

Yield: 10 to 16 servings.

Chive-Cheese

1 12-ounce carton (1½ cups) chive cream-style cottage cheese
3 to 6 drops Tabasco sauce

Place cheese and Tabasco sauce in blender; blend until fluffy and creamy.

Chopped parsley or chives

Garnish with parsley or chives.
Serve with potato chips, pretzels, or crackers.

Yield: 1½ cups.

Chili Dip

⅔ cup low-fat cottage cheese
⅓ cup chili sauce
1 teaspoon chili powder
1½ teaspoons prepared horseradish
½ teaspoon salt
⅔ cup plain yogurt

Blend cottage cheese and chili sauce together in small bowl until fairly smooth.

Add chili powder, horseradish, and salt.

Fold in yogurt. Cover; chill several hours.

Yield: about 1⅔ cups.

Smoky Cheese Dip

1 cup cottage cheese, creamed
1 tablespoon milk
⅛ teaspoon onion salt
1 teaspoon vinegar
¼ cup or 2 ounces smoke-flavored process cheese food, shredded

Beat all ingredients together or mix in blender.

Yield: about 1⅓ cups.

Crab-Meat Spread

1 can (7½ ounces) king crab meat, drained, flaked
1 teaspoon prepared horseradish
½ teaspoon seasoned salt
¼ teaspoon lemon juice
Dash white pepper
½ cup plain yogurt

Combine crab meat, horseradish, seasoned salt, lemon juice, and pepper.

Fold in yogurt.
Cover; chill.

Use to spread on crackers or as dip.

Yield: About 1¼ cups.

Crab Meat Nibbles

4 slices bread **Butter**	Remove crusts from bread; toast on one side only. Lightly butter untoasted side.
1 can (about 6 ounces) crab meat	Flake crab meat.
2 teaspoons mayonnaise **1 teaspoon grated onion** **½ cup grated cheddar or American cheese** **Preheat broiler.**	Combine with mayonnaise and onion. Spread on buttered side of toast. Sprinkle generously with cheese. Put under hot broiler 1 to 2 minutes, until cheese melts and is lightly browned. Serve at once. Yield: 4 servings.

Garlic Bread

1 long loaf French bread	Cut French loaf into slanting slices without quite cutting through bottom of loaf.
3 to 4 tablespoons butter **1 to 2 cloves garlic** **Salt and pepper to taste** **1 teaspoon oregano (optional)**	Soften butter; mix in crushed garlic and seasonings. Spread mixture between slices. Close loaf; wrap in foil. Put into medium oven to heat through, about 10 minutes. Open foil; allow bread to crisp about 2 minutes. Yield: 20 slices.

Hot Dogs in Brandy

Can be made directly in chafing dish or done in skillet on stove, your choice.

½ cup brown sugar **½ cup soy sauce** **¼ cup brandy**	Mix sugar, soy sauce, and brandy until blended and hot, 3 to 5 minutes.
1 12-ounce package cocktail hot dogs	Add hot dogs; simmer together 10 minutes. Have toothpicks handy so hot dogs can be removed from sauce to be eaten. Yield: Never quite enough, as these are so popular.

SALADS

Apple and Cheese Salad

3-ounce package lime- or
  lemon-flavored gelatin
1 cup boiling water
1 cup cold water
3-ounce package cream
  cheese, room temperature
1 cup unpaired, finely
  diced apple
1 cup seedless grapes
¼ cup chopped pecans

Several lettuce leaves

Dissolve gelatin in boiling water; add cold water.
Chill until thick but not set.

Add cream cheese; beat with rotary beater until well
  blended.
Stir in apples, grapes, and pecans.
Pour into 1-quart ring mold.
Chill until firm.

Unmold on lettuce.

Yield: 6 servings.

Crunchy Pear Salad

3 cups diced Anjou pears
1 cup shredded carrots
⅓ cup raisins
⅓ cup chopped nuts

Combine pears, carrots, raisins, and nuts.

⅔ cup mayonnaise
1 tablespoon lemon juice
⅛ teaspoon salt

Blend mayonnaise with lemon juice and salt.
Add to salad, mix well.

Yield: 6 servings.

Marinated Bean Salad

¼ cup oil
1 tablespoon sugar
1 tablespoon vinegar
1 tablespoon Worcestershire
  sauce
¼ teaspoon salt
1 can (1 pound) cut green
  beans, drained
1 can (1 pound) cut wax
  beans, drained

Combine oil, sugar, vinegar, Worcestershire sauce, and salt;
  pour over beans.
Toss gently.

Lettuce
Sliced onion, if desired

Serve on lettuce garnished with onion.

Yield: 6 servings.

Cucumber Salad

3 tablespoons boiling water
½ cup vinegar
3 tablespoons sugar
½ teaspoon salt
½ teaspoon freshly-
  ground pepper

Combine all ingredients except cucumbers in saucepan.
Bring to boil.

3 cucumbers
Parsley

Thinly slice, but do not peel, cucumbers.
Pour liquid over cucumbers. Allow to cool.

Serve salad garnished with parsley.

Yield: 6 to 8 servings.

Turkey or Chicken Salad

3 cups diced cooked turkey
  or chicken
1 cup diced celery
½ teaspoon salt
⅛ teaspoon pepper
1 tablespoon minced onion
1 tablespoon lemon juice, if
  desired
½ cup mayonnaise or salad
  dressing or ⅓ cup French
  dressing

Mix all ingredients gently.
Chill before serving.

Yield: 6 servings.

Turkey or chicken and Fruit Salad.

Add 1 cup seedless grapes or pineapple chunks.

Artichoke and Tomato Salad

2 4-ounce jars marinated
  artichoke hearts

Drain artichoke hearts; reserve marinade. Cut artichoke
  hearts in half; place in large salad bowl.

½ cup sauterne
Juice of 1 lemon

Combine reserved marinade, wine, and lemon juice; pour
  over artichoke hearts.

1 whole fennel*
6 medium tomatoes, sliced
2 small onions, diced
1 clove garlic
½ teaspoon salt
¼ teaspoon white pepper
½ cup warm beef broth

Clean fennel. *Wash; slice. Add to artichoke hearts.
Add tomatoes and onions.

Mash garlic clove with salt and pepper; add to beef broth.
Mix well; pour over vegetables.
Marinate at least 10 minutes.

Serve with crusty bread.

Yield: 6 to 8 servings.

*If fennel unavailable, substitue 1 small bunch celery,
  cleaned and sliced.

Shrimp Plate

3 cans (4½ or 5 ounces
  each) shrimp

1 large cucumber, sliced
Lettuce
Shrimp Sauce

Drain shrimp. Cover with ice water; let stand 5 minutes;
  drain.
Arrange shrimp and cucumber slices on lettuce.
Serve with Shrimp Sauce.

Shrimp Sauce

1 cup sour cream
1 tablespoon horseradish
1 tablespoon grated onion
½ teaspoon paprika
½ teaspoon salt

Combine all ingredients; blend well.

Yield: 6 servings.

Peaches Filled with Cheese

1 can (about 30 ounces)
  peach halves
3 tablespoons grated
  cheddar cheese
1 tablespoon grated
  parmesan cheese
1 tablespoon softened butter
Salt
Cayenne pepper

Drain peaches.

Mix cheese with butter; season to taste with salt and
  pepper. Fill peach halves.

Lettuce

Arrange on platter or on individual dishes on lettuce bed.

1 package (3 ounces) cream
  cheese
5 to 6 tablespoons light
  cream
Paprika

Beat cream-cheese and light cream together. Spoon over
  peaches.

Sprinkle with paprika.

Yield: 4 to 5 servings.

Peaches Filled with Cheese

SOUP

Beet Borscht

1 ¼-inch-thick lemon slice,
   rind and seeds removed
1 cup diced cooked beets
½ medium onion, chopped
1¾ cups sour cream
¼ teaspoon salt
1 cup crushed ice

Place all ingredients except ice in blender; blend 20
   seconds.
Add ice; blend 30 seconds.

Serve borscht in soup cups or small bowls; garnish with
   dollop of sour cream.

Yield: about 4 servings.

Beet Borscht

Chilled Spinach Soup

2 cups chicken bouillon
1 10-ounce package frozen
   chopped spinach

1 cup yogurt

Bring bouillon to boil in saucepan.
Add frozen spinach; bring to second boil. Break spinach
   apart with a fork. Simmer 3 minutes.

Puree mixture in blender, a portion at a time.
Add yogurt to one portion while blending.
Blend portions together.
Chill before serving.

Yield: 6 servings.

Cream of Corn Soup

3 tablespoons butter
1 onion, chopped
1 medium potato, finely
   sliced
1½ cups fresh or canned
   corn
3½ cups milk
1 bay leaf
3 to 4 parsley sprigs
Salt and pepper to taste
¼ teaspoon mace
1 chicken-stock cube

4 to 6 spoons heavy cream
1 tablespoon chopped chives
   or parsley (or sprinkling of
   paprika)
Fried bread croutons

Melt butter; cook onion and potato gently with lid on pan
   5 minutes. Shake pan occasionally to prevent sticking.

Add 1 cup corn; stir well.

Add milk, bay leaf, parsley, salt, pepper, and mace.
Bring to simmer.

Add chicken-stock cube.
Cook until vegetables are tender.

Put soup into electric blender and blend until smooth; or
   put through fine food mill.
Return soup to pan with remaining corn (which, if fresh,
   should be simmered in salted water until tender). Reheat
   soup until nearly boiling; adjust seasoning.
Serve in soup cups with spoonful of cream in each cup,
   sprinkling of chives, parsley, and croutons.

Yield: 4 to 6 servings.

Cream of Corn Soup

Asparagus Soup

1 8-ounce can cut asparagus
   spears
1 cup chicken broth
Salt and white pepper to
   taste
Fresh parsley, minced

In blender puree asparagus spears with their liquid and
   chicken broth.

Heat, adding salt and pepper.

Sprinkle with parsley.

Serve hot.

Yield: 4 servings.

Tomato Consommé

2 cans jellied condensed
  consommé

Heat consommé very slightly to dissolve.

1 small bottle tomato juice
  cocktail with Tobasco or
  Worcestershire sauce
  added

Add tomato juice and curry powder. Mix in thoroughly.

2 teaspoons curry powder
  (or paste)

Few drops lemon juice

Add a little lemon juice.
Pour into soup cups; let chill.
Mix mayonnaise with grated lemon rind and juice.

3 tablespoons fresh
  mayonnaise

Grated lemon rind to taste

1 to 2 teaspoons lemon juice

1 tablespoon heavy cream,
  whipped

Add whipped cream.
Put spoonful of this mayonnaise onto center of each cup
  of soup; sprinkle with chopped chives.

2 teaspoons chopped chives

Serve with brown bread and butter.

Yield: 4 to 6 servings.

Tomato Consommé

14

Zucchini Soup

1 medium onion, chopped
1 tablespoon
  polyunsaturated
  margarine

In large frypan sauté onion in hot margarine.

4 to 6 medium zucchini,
  sliced
1 large potato, peeled, diced
¼ teaspoon thyme
¼ teaspoon rosemary
¼ teaspoon basil
¼ teaspoon salt
⅛ teaspoon pepper
6 cups chicken broth

Add zucchini, potato, herbs, salt, and pepper.
After mixture is hot, cook 3 minutes; stir occasionally.
Add chicken broth; simmer 15 minutes.

Add chicken broth; simmer 15 minutes.

Puree in blender.
Return mixture to saucepan. Add milk; heat slightly.

1 cup skim milk

Serve hot or cold.

Yield: 8 servings.

Cream of Mushroom Soup

4 tablespoons butter
1 onion, chopped

Melt butter; cook onion 4 to 5 minutes to soften.

2 to 3 cups sliced
  mushrooms

Add mushrooms. Cover pan; cook 5 minutes.

3 tablespoons flour
3 cups chicken or white
  stock (or water and cube)

Sprinkle in flour; stir until smooth.
Pour on stock; mix well.

1 bay leaf
3 to 4 sprigs parsley
¼ teaspoon mace
Salt and pepper to taste

Add bay leaf, parsley, and mace.

Season with salt and pepper.
Bring to boil; simmer 10 to 15 minutes.
Remove bay leaf. Put soup through fine food mill or into
  electric blender; blend until smooth.

2 cups creamy milk
Chopped parsley or chives
Fried bread croutons

Reheat; add heated milk. Adjust seasoning to taste.
Sprinkle with parsley.
Serve with croutons.

Yield: 4 to 6 servings.

Italian Stracciatella

2 large or 3 small eggs
Salt and pepper to taste
½ cup grated Parmesan or
  other hard, well-flavored
  cheese

Beat eggs well with a little salt and pepper; stir in grated cheese.

5 cups well-flavored clear
  chicken stock

Strain chicken stock into pan, after removing any traces of fat.
Bring to boil, skimming if necessary.
When boiling fast, pour in cheese and egg mixture slowly with one hand; whisk soup with other hand. Allow soup to cook gently a few minutes.

1 tablespoon chopped
  parsley

Serve at once sprinkled with parsley.

1 glass white wine (optional)

A little white wine can be added to soup if desired.

Yield: 4 to 6 servings.

Oyster Stew

1 can (12 ounces) oysters,
  fresh or frozen

Thaw frozen oysters. Drain oysters, reserving liquor.

2 cups oyster liquor and
  water
1 package (1¾ ounces)
  cream of leek soup mix

Add oyster liquor and water to soup mix; bring to boil, stirring constantly. Reduce heat; simmer 10 minutes.

1 cup milk

Add milk; heat, stirring occasionally.
Add oysters; heat 3 to 5 minutes longer, until edges of oysters begin to curl.

1 tablespoon chopped
  parsley

Sprinkle with parsley.

Yield: 6 servings.

Mock Crab Bisque

1 can tomato soup
1 can green pea soup
1 can milk or light cream

Mix cans of soup in electric blender; slowly add milk.
Put into soup pot; heat without boiling.

1 small can crab meat or
  shrimp

When really hot, add crab meat. Reheat; add sherry and butter at last minute.

2 to 3 tablespoons sherry
1 tablespoon butter
4 to 6 tablespoons heavy
  cream

Serve hot with spoonful of heavy cream in each cup.

1 tablespoon chopped
  parsley or sprinkling of
  paprika

Sprinkle with parsley.

Yield: 4 to 6 servings.

MEAT

Bacon-Crust Pie

Bacon Crust

2 cups ground lean bacon
1 small can tomato puree
½ cup bread crumbs
1 small onion, very finely chopped
¼ cup chopped green pepper

Preheat oven to 375°F.

Mix all ingredients for crust together; knead well.
Press into bottom of 8- or 9-inch pie plate. Flute around edge.

Filling

1 cup cooked rice
1 small can tomato puree
⅛ teaspoon oregano
Salt and pepper to taste
1¼ cups grated Gruyere cheese

Mix rice, tomato puree, oregano, salt, pepper, and 1 cup cheese. Spoon into pie shell. Cover with waxed paper.

Bake 15 to 20 minutes.
Remove paper; sprinkle with remaining cheese.
Brown lightly under hot broiler.

Yield: 4 or 5 servings.

Bacon with Parsley Sauce

Parsley Sauce

3 tablespoons butter
1 tablespoon finely chopped onion
1½ tablespoons flour
1 cup milk

Make sauce: Melt butter; cook onion few minutes with lid on pan.

Add flour; mix well.
Add warmed milk; mix until smooth before returning to stove. Bring slowly to boil, stirring constantly. Boil 2 minutes.

4 to 6 tablespoons chopped parsley
Pinch of nutmeg
1 tablespoon cream (optional)
12 to 16 slices lean bacon

Add parsley, salt, pepper, and nutmeg. (If using cream, add now.)

Remove rind from bacon; broil or fry until crisp.

Serve bacon hot with good helping parsley sauce for each serving.

Yield: 4 servings.

Beef with Bean Sprouts and Mushrooms

2 tablespoons vegetable oil
¼ pound mushrooms, cut
    into "T" shapes
1 teaspoon grated fresh
    gingerroot
1 pound beef (round, chuck,
    flank) finely sliced

Heat oil in wok or skillet. Stir-fry mushrooms and grated
    ginger 1 to 2 minutes; push aside.
Stir-fry beef 3 to 4 minutes.
Return mushrooms to beef in wok.

2 tablespoons soy sauce
2 tablespoons dry sherry
½ cup chicken broth or
    water
1 tablespoon cornstarch in 2
    tablespoons water
1 or 2 cups bean sprouts

Combine soy sauce, sherry, broth, and cornstarch mixture.
Stir; add to beef and mushrooms. Heat until sauce
    thickens.

Add bean sprouts; continue heating just until they are
    heated through.

2 stalks celery, cut into
    small cubes

Garnish with celery; serve at once with rice.

Yield: 4 servings.

Beef and Macaroni Stew

1 tablespoon butter or oil
1 pound ground beef
½ cup chopped onion
1 clove garlic
1 small green pepper,
    chopped
1 large can tomatoes
1 cup uncooked macaroni
2 teaspoons salt
¼ teaspoon pepper
½ to ¾ cup stock or water
2 tablespoons chopped
    parsley and thyme

Melt butter.
Add meat; brown gently all over about 10 minutes.
Add onion, garlic, pepper, tomatoes, macaroni (broken into
    small pieces), seasoning stock, and half the herbs.
Mix in well.

Cook in covered pan, stirring occasionally 20 to 30
    minutes, until macaroni is soft.

Sprinkle remaining herbs on top. Serve.

Yield: 4 servings.

Beef Casserole

1 pound round steak, cut
   into bite-size pieces
1 can cream of chicken soup
1 can cream of mushroom
   soup
1 small can whole
   mushrooms
½ package dried onion soup
   mix
½ cup sherry wine

Place meat in casserole dish.

Mix all other ingredients; pour over meat. Cover.

Bake 3 hours in 350°F oven.

Serve over noodles or rice.

Yield: 6 servings.

Beef and Mushroom Pie

Preheat oven to 425°F.

Pastry for an 8- to 9-inch
   2-crust pie

Line 8-inch pie plate with half the pastry.

2 tablespoons butter or
   margarine
1 tablespoon corn oil
2 small onions, peeled,
   finely chopped
1 cup sliced mushrooms
2 tablespoons flour
1 beef bouillon cube,
   crumbled

Heat butter and corn oil in sauté pan.

Add onions and mushrooms.

Cook until lightly browned.
Stir in flour and bouillon cube. Add 1 cup water; stir until
   boiling.

1½ cups ground cooked
   beef
2 teaspoons finely chopped
   parsley
1 teaspoon prepared
   horseradish
Salt and pepper

Remove from heat; stir in meat, parsley, and horseradish.
   Check seasoning.

Milk

Put into pastry shell; cover with rest of pastry. Press edges
   well together.
Decorate edge; brush with milk.

Bake 20 to 30 minutes.

Yield: 4 or 5 servings.

Beef and Rice Ragout

Beef and Rice Ragout

1 small onion, chopped
1 green pepper, chopped
1 tablespoon oil
1 pound lean ground beef or veal
1 teaspoon salt
Dash of black pepper

Use medium to large skillet.
Stir onion and green pepper in oil until soft.
Add ground meat, salt, and pepper; stir until meat loses pink color.

1 tablespoon prepared mustard
2 tablespoons catsup
1 tablespoon Worcestershire sauce
3 cups cooked rice
3 cups canned tomatoes

Add remaining ingredients; stir until well blended. Reduce heat; cover skillet.

Simmer just 15 minutes.

Yield: 4 to 6 servings.

20

Stuffed Zucchini

4 medium zucchini squash
  (about 2 pounds total)

1 pound ground beef
¼ cup olive oil
2 cloves garlic, minced
1 medium chopped onion
½ cup chopped green
  pepper
1 teaspoon crushed dried
  mint
1 cup fresh bread crumbs
1 tablespoon chopped
  parsley
1¾ cups tomato sauce
¼ cup grated Kafaloteri
  cheese
Salt and pepper

Slice zucchini in half lengthwise. Scoop out pulp; chop.

Sauté ground beef in oil until it loses pink color.

Add garlic, onion, and green pepper; cook 5 minutes.
  Remove from heat.

Add zucchini pulp, mint, bread crumbs, parsley, ¼ cup
  tomato sauce, cheese, and salt and pepper to taste.

Stuff squash shells with mixture. Put squash in 13 × 9 ×
  2-inch baking dish.
Pour remaining 1½ cups tomato sauce over squash.

Bake at 350°F 40 minutes.

Yield: 4 servings.

Stuffed Zucchini

21

Beef Pie

1½ pounds ground beef
1 medium-size onion,
    chopped
½ teaspoon salt

Crumble beef into large frypan.
Add onion and salt; cook until browned. Drain off excess
    fat.

1 can (10½ ounces)
    condensed tomato soup
1 can (16 ounces) cut green
    beans, drained
¼ teaspoon pepper

Add soup, beans, and pepper; simmer 5 minutes.
Pour into greased 2-quart casserole.

1½ cups seasoned mashed
    potatoes
½ cup shredded cheddar
    cheese

Drop potatoes in mounds onto hot meat mixture.

Sprinkle with cheese. Bake at 350°F 20 minutes.

Yield: 6 servings.

Cheeseburgers

Preheat broiler.

1 onion
2 tablespoons oil
½ cup mushrooms
1 pound ground round steak
1 teaspoon mixed herbs
2 teaspoons chutney
Salt and pepper

Cook chopped onion in hot oil until soft, about 4 minutes.

Add chopped mushrooms; cook 2 to 3 minutes.
Add steak, herbs, chutney, and seasoning. Mix well.

4 slices processed cheese,
    cut in half

8 hamburger buns

Divide into 8 round flat cakes; brush with oil.

Broil each side 5 to 6 minutes.

Put slice of cheese on top each beefburger.
Broil another 2 minutes.

Put into slit-open buns; eat at once.

Yield: 4 servings.

Chili Con Carne

This recipe can be made using a package of chili seasoning, with canned meat and tomatoes. The cooking time can then be cut to half an hour.

2 tablespoons bacon fat
1 onion, chopped
1 to 2 cloves garlic, crushed
1½ pounds ground beef

2 to 3 cups canned cooked
   red kidney beans
1 pound tomatoes, peeled,
   chopped
¾ cup beef stock
1 to 2 tablespoons chili
   powder
1 bay leaf
1 teaspoon sugar
Salt and pepper

Melt bacon fat. Add onion and garlic.
Cook 5 minutes.

Add meat; cook another 2 to 3 minutes.

Mix in canned beans, tomatoes, stock, chili powder, bay leaf, sugar, salt, and pepper.

Cover pan with lid.

Cook slowly about 1 hour.

Yield: 4 to 6 servings.

Corned-Beef–Stuffed Green Peppers

Preheat oven to 375°F.

3 large green peppers

¼ cup onion, chopped
2 tablespoons butter or
   margarine
1 tablespoon prepared
   horseradish
2 cans (16 ounces each)
   corned-beef hash

Cut peppers in half. Remove seeds.
Cook 10 minutes in boiling water to cover. Drain.

Cook onion in butter just until tender.

Stir in horseradish.

Mix with hash.

Fill pepper halves with hash mixture.
Place peppers in baking dish. Pour in 1 cup water.

Bake 30 minutes.

Yield: 6 servings.

Ground-Beef Gumbo

1 large onion, sliced
1 tablespoon shortening
1½ pounds ground beef

1 can chicken-gumbo soup
   (condensed)
1 teaspoon salt
¼ teaspoon freshly ground
   black pepper

Tan onion in hot shortening in medium skillet.

Add ground beef; stir until all is browned.

Add soup, (without water), salt, and pepper. Simmer about 5 minutes or until all flavors blend.

Serve on hamburger rolls.

Yield: 4 to 6 servings.

Ground-Beef Stroganoff

1 pound ground beef
¼ cups chopped onion
1 crushed garlic clove
1 can condensed cream of
   mushroom soup
⅓ cup milk
2 tablespoons sherry
½ cup sour cream
Salt and pepper

Cooked noodles or rice
Chopped parsley

Lightly brown meat in skillet with onion and garlic, stirring.

Add soup and milk; heat well, stirring.
Reduce heat.

Stir in sherry, then sour cream. Season to taste.

Serve over noodles, with parsley for garnish.

Yield: 4 to 6 servings.

Skillet Dinner

1 pound ground beef
4 ounces macaroni, cooked,
   drained
1 can tomato puree
½ can water
¼ teaspoon each oregano,
   sweet basil and salt
½ onion, chopped
2 cloves garlic, crushed

Brown ground beef in skillet; drain off fat.
Add rest of ingredients. Simmer, covered, 10 to 20 minutes; stir occasionally.

Can be served topped with 1 cup grated cheese.

Yield: 3 to 4 servings.

Steak Diane

3 tablespoons chopped
    scallions
3 tablespoons vegetable oil
3 tablespoons finely
    chopped chives
3 tablespoons finely
    chopped parsley
1 tablespoon Worcestershire
    sauce
½ teaspoon salt
¼ teaspoon pepper

Sauté scallions in 1 tablespoon hot oil for minute or two.

Add chives, parsley, Worcestershire sauce, salt, and
    pepper.

4 beef steaks, fillets, or rib-
    eye steaks

In second frypan sauté steaks with remaining 2 table-
    spoons hot oil until done. (Time depends on thickness of
    steak.)
Top each steak with some scallion mixture.

¼ cup brandy, warmed

Flame with warmed brandy until alcohol content is com-
    pletely burned.

Spoon pan juices over steaks; serve.

Yield: 4 servings.

Toad in the Hole

1½ pounds good beefsteak,
    cubed
Salt and pepper

Cut beefsteak into cubes about inch square (a few large).
Season cubes well with salt and pepper; place in shallow
    baking dish, well greased.
Spread cubes apart so batter can go between.

2 eggs
1 cup flour
½ teaspoon salt
2 cups milk

Make batter of remaining ingredients. Pour over beef
    cubes; make some larger cubes have "heads" stuck out
    of batter.

Bake in hot oven 30 minutes.

Yield: 4 servings.

Baked Beans and Frankfurters

1½ teaspoons butter or
   margarine

Melt butter in medium skillet.

6 frankfurters
2 teaspoons minced onion
¼ teaspoon instant minced
   garlic
¼ teaspoon crumbled dried
   leaf oregano

Sauté frankfurters, onion, garlic, and oregano, stirring often
   to brown evenly.

1 can (28-ounce) brickoven
   baked beans
1 medium tomato

Add baked beans.
Heat thoroughly.
Add tomato, cut in thin wedges.
Heat several minutes.

Yield: 4 or 5 servings.

Ham and Cheese Toast

4 slices cooked ham
4 slices buttered toast
A little chopped chutney
4 slices Gruyere cheese

Put slice of ham on each piece of toast. Spread lightly with
   chutney; cover with slice of cheese.

2 tomatoes, peeled, sliced

Arrange tomato slices on top.

Put under hot broiler to heat through.

Yield: 4 servings.

Hasty Hash

1 can condensed mushroom
   soup
¼ cup milk

Mix soup and milk in medium skillet until well blended.
Add ham, egg slices, and seasonings.

1 cup cubed, cooked ham or
   other leftover meat
2 sliced hard-cooked eggs
Salt and pepper to taste

Heat mixture over very low heat until blended.

Triangles of toast

Spoon mixture over toast triangles; serve.

Yield: 4 to 6 servings.

Pepper Steaks

Pepper Steaks

Preheat broiler.

4 large sirloin steaks (1 inch thick)
2 tablespoons peppercorns, crushed

Press pepper well into steaks, using wooden spoon.

3 to 4 tablespoons oil
¼ cup butter

Heat oil in pan; add half of butter.
When foaming, fry steaks 4 to 6 minutes on each side, longer if preferred.
Add remaining butter, if needed. Remove to heated dish to keep warm.

½ cup white wine
2 tablespoons brandy (optional)
Little lemon juice
Salt and pepper

Add wine, brandy, and lemon juice to juices in pan.
Bring to boil; season with salt and pepper. Pour over steaks.

Serve at once.

The pepper can be scraped off before adding sauce, if preferred.

Yield: 4 servings.

Marinated Steak

1 to 1½ pounds filet mignon or round steak.

marinade

Cut filet mignon into thin slices.

4 tablespoons sherry
4 tablespoons soy sauce
1½ heaping tablespoons
   cornstarch
Salt
Pinch of sugar
Pinch of white pepper

Prepare marinade by stirring sherry, soy sauce, cornstarch, a little salt, sugar, and pepper thoroughly until well blended.

Pour marinade over meat slices; marinate 1 hour.

4 tablespoons oil

Heat oil in heavy skillet until very hot.

Add meat, including marinade; cook 5 minutes, stirring constantly.

Serve steak immediately.

Yield: 4 servings.

Marinated Steak

Glazed Mushrooms and Ham

¼ cup butter	Melt butter in pan.
⅓ cup brown sugar	Add sugar and flour mixed together; stir over low heat until sugar has melted.
1 teaspoon flour	
4 cups thickly sliced mushrooms	Add mushrooms, nutmeg, and mace. Cover; cook very slowly 5 minutes.
¼ teaspoon grated nutmeg	
¼ teaspoon ground mace	
4 to 6 slices cooked ham	Uncover; arrange ham over mushrooms.
	Increase heat just long enough for ham to heat through.
3 tablespoons sherry	Add sherry; turn upside down on hot serving dish.

Yield: 4 servings.

Curried Meat

2 beef bouillon cubes	Dissolve bouillon cubes in hot water.
1⅓ cups hot water	
1½ cups sliced celery	Lightly brown celery and onion in hot fat in large frypan.
2 tablespoons chopped onion	
3 tablespoons fat or oil	
1 tablespoon cornstarch	Blend in cornstarch and seasonings.
1 teaspoon curry powder	Slowly stir in bouillon.
½ teaspoon salt	
3 cups cooked lamb, pork, or veal, chopped	Add meat.
	Cook over moderate heat 15 to 20 minutes; stir as needed to prevent sticking.

Serve on rice.

Yield: 6 servings.

Liver with Rice

Liver with Rice

½ to ¾ **pound lamb or calf liver**	Cut liver into chunks.
1 onion	Chop onion fine.
1 clove garlic	Crush garlic.
	Quarter mushrooms.
2 to 3 tablespoons butter	Melt butter; cook onion and garlic few minutes with lid on pan.
	Add liver; cook quickly until it changes color.
	Remove from heat.
1 cup quartered mushrooms	Add mushrooms, rice, tomato puree, 2½ cups stock, salt, and pepper.
1 cup long-grain rice	
1 dessert spoon tomato puree	Bring to boil, stirring all the time.
2½ to 3 cups stock	Reduce heat; simmer gently 25 to 30 minutes, stirring occasionally. Add extra stock if rice seems to be getting dry.
Salt and pepper	When cooked, rice should have absorbed all moisture.
1 tablespoon mixed herbs	Sprinkle top with chopped herbs.
1 cup grated Parmesan cheese	Serve with grated cheese.
	Yield: 4 servings.

Lamb with Rice

This recipe puts a leftover roast to good use.

¼ cup butter or margarine	Melt butter in large saucepan.
½ cup chopped onion	Add chopped onion; cook until limp.
1½ cups raw long-grain rice	Add rice; cook 4 to 5 minutes, until lightly colored, stirring frequently.
3 cups boiling water 3 teaspoons instant chicken broth, granulated 1 teaspoon dried mint	Add boiling water, chicken broth, and dried mint. Cover; reduce heat to simmer. Cook 15 minutes.
2 cups cubed cooked lamb ½ cup golden raisins	Add lamb and raisins; cook 5 minutes, until all liquid is absorbed.
2 tablespoons chopped parsley	Fluff; serve garnished with parsley. Yield: 4 servings.

Liver and Peppers

2 tablespoons butter or margarine	Heat butter in large skillet.
3 large green peppers, cut into ½-inch strips 4 slices calves' liver, ½ inch thick	Cook pepper strips until tender, about 10 minutes. Remove peppers from skillet to platter to keep warm.
2 tablespoons flour 1 teaspoon salt 1 teaspoon paprika	Mix flour, salt, and paprika on waxed paper. Coat each liver slice with mixture. Place floured liver slices in same skillet; add more butter if needed. Cook until crisp and brown on outside, 2 to 4 minutes per side.
1 teaspoon lemon juice Green-pepper strips for garnish	Sprinkle cooked liver with lemon juice. Serve surrounded by pepper strips. Yield: 4 servings

Liver with Vegetables

1 medium onion, chopped
Cooking oil

In skillet cook onion in oil until tender. Remove onions from skillet.

1 tablespoon flour
1 teaspoon paprika
1 pound calves' liver
2 (1-pound) cans stewed
   tomatoes
1½ (12-ounce) cans whole-
   kernel corn, drained
½ teaspoon salt

Mix flour and paprika together; dip liver in mixture.
Add liver to skillet; brown lightly on each side.

Add onions, tomatoes, corn, and salt.
Simmer gently about 3 minutes, until liver is tender.

Yield: About 4 servings.

Liver with Beer

¼ pound butter or
   margarine
1 medium onion, chopped
   fine

Melt butter in medium skillet; cook onion until transparent.

¼ teaspoon garlic powder
1½ pounds chicken livers
1 tablespoon flour
½ cup beer

Add garlic powder and chicken livers; cook until livers brown on all sides.
Mix flour with 1 tablespoon beer; add to livers. Stirring constantly, add rest of beer until sauce thickens and livers are done through, about 5 minutes.

3 cups cooked rice

Put hot cooked rice in center of platter; mound chicken livers around it.

Yield: 4 to 6 servings.

Onion Pork Chops

4 to 6 large pork chops
1 (10½-ounce) can con-
   densed onion soup

In medium skillet lightly brown pork chops in own fat.
When both sides are browned, add onion soup.
Cover; reduce heat to simmer.
Cook slowly 1 hour.

Yield: 4 to 6 servings

Sausage Pie

Preheat oven to 450°F.

Pastry for an 8- to 9-inch 1-crust pie

Line 8- to 9-inch pie plate with pastry; prick bottom.

¾ cup butter or margarine
1 small onion, peeled, chopped
4 tablespoons chopped cooked ham
1 cup sliced mushrooms

Bake 10 to 15 minutes; remove from oven.
Heat ¼ cup butter in small pan.
Sauté onion, ham, and mushrooms until onion is transparent; set aside.

1 tablespoon flour
1 cup milk
Salt and pepper
⅛ teaspoon grated nutmeg
1 egg yolk
2 tablespoons heavy cream

Make sauce with ¼ cup butter, flour, and milk.

When smooth and thickened, add salt, pepper, and nutmeg.
Remove from heat; stir in egg yolk and cream.

8 small link sausages

2 to 3 tablespoons grated cheese

Sauté sausages in remaining butter until lightly brown.
Put onion and ham mixture into pie shell.
Arrange sausages in spoke fashion on top. Pour sauce over; sprinkle with cheese.

Bake about 20 minutes.

Yield: 4 or 5 servings.

Stuffed Sausageburgers

Preheat oven to 350°F.

1 pound skinless pork sausages
A little fat

Brush sausages with fat.

Broil 7 to 10 minutes, until cooked all over. Keep warm.

8 hamburger rolls
4 tablespoons butter
1 teaspoon mustard

Split rolls; spread with half of butter and mustard.

2 to 3 tablespoons grated cheddar cheese
1 tablespoon chutney

Mix cheese with rest of butter and chutney.

Split sausages lengthwise; fill with mixture.
Put one sausage in each bun.
Put in oven; warm through.

Yield: 4 servings.

Veal Scallops

4 pieces veal scallops 2 tablespoons flour	Pound veal until very thin (⅛-inch). Dredge lightly in flour, shaking off excess.
4 tablespoons corn-oil margarine	In skillet, melt 3 tablespoons margarine.
1 clove garlic	Crush garlic clove; place in skillet until golden brown. Discard clove. Place veal in skillet; cook quickly, just until brown, about 1 to 2 minutes on each side. Remove onto serving dish.
¼ cup dry vermouth 1 tablespoon lemon juice	Add remaining margarine, wine, and lemon juice to skillet. Simmer 3 minutes, scraping bottom of pan to loosen drippings. Pour sauce over veal.
½ lemon, sliced	Garnish with lemon slices; serve. Yield: 4 servings.

Veal Scallops Parmesan

4 thin veal scallops (or slices cut from leg of veal)	Beat scallops between waxed paper.
1 large egg ½ tablespoon oil Salt and pepper ½ teaspoon powdered garlic 3 tablespoons flour 3 to 4 tablespoons grated Parmesan cheese	Mix egg with oil; beat. Add seasoning and garlic to flour; mix with cheese. Brush scallops with egg mixture; press into cheese and flour until completely coated.
3 tablespoons butter	Melt butter; fry scallops until golden brown, about 5 to 6 minutes each side. Place on warm serving dish; keep hot.
Juice of ½ lemon	Add lemon juice to butter in pan. Reheat; pour over scallops just before serving.
1 tablespoon finely chopped parsley	Decorate with parsley. Yield: 4 servings.

Chicken Oregano

POULTRY

Chicken Oregano

3 pounds fryer-chicken parts **1 large freezer bag**	Wash chicken parts; pat dry. Place in freezer bag.
½ cup olive oil **¼ cup lemon juice** **2 cloves garlic, minced** **½ teaspoon salt** **1 teaspoon crumbled dried oregano** **½ teaspoon freshly ground pepper**	Combine oil, lemon juice, garlic, salt, oregano, and pepper; pour over chicken. Tie bag shut; turn several times to coat chicken with marinade. Refrigerate 24 hours, turning bag occasionally.
	cooking Remove chicken from bag; reserve marinade.
2 tablespoons butter, melted	Grill, 5 inches from white-hot charcoal, 30 minutes; turn once. Brush frequently with reserved marinade combined with butter. Yield: 4 or 5 servings.
	variation Substitute 1 3-pound roasting chicken for chicken parts. Marinate in same manner. Drain chicken; reserve marinade. Mount on rotisserie spit; cook 1½ hours on indoor unit or over charcoal. Baste frequently with marinade mixed with butter.

Chicken with Peppers and Cashews

2 tablespoons vegetable oil
1 large green pepper, cut
 into ¼-inch strips
4 chicken-breast halves,
 skinned, boned, cut into
 ½-inch strips
2 tablespoons soy sauce
1 tablespoon cornstarch
½ cup cold chicken broth
2 tablespoons dry white
 wine
½ cup cashews

Heat oil in wok or skillet. Add peppers; stir-fry 2 minutes.
 Push aside.

Stir-fry chicken 3 to 4 minutes, until done.
Return peppers to chicken in wok.

Combine; stir in soy sauce, cornstarch, chicken broth, and
 wine.
Heat; stir gently until sauce is thickened and clear.

Add cashews.

Serve at once with rice.

Yield: 4 servings.

Chicken with Peppers and Cashews

Oriental Chicken

¼ cup orange marmalade
1 package dry onion soup
 mix
1 frying chicken, quartered

Blend marmalade and soup mix in small bowl.

Place chicken in baking dish; dab sauce evenly on each
 piece.

Cook in 325°F oven 1 hour, until tender.

Yield: 4 servings.

Chicken with Celery and Mushrooms

2 tablespoons vegetable oil
3 to 4 stalks celery, cut into ¼-inch slices
¼ pound whole small mushrooms
1 broiler-fryer chicken, skinned, boned, cut into ½-inch strips
½ cup chicken broth or water
1 tablespoon soy sauce
1 tablespoon cornstarch in 2 tablespoons water
¼ cup dry sherry

Heat oil in wok or skillet; stir-fry celery and mushrooms 2 to 3 minutes. Push aside.

Stir-fry chicken 3 to 4 minutes, until done.
Combine chicken and vegetables.

Add broth, soy sauce, cornstarch mixture, and sherry.
Heat until sauce boils and is thickened; stir constantly.

Serve at once with rice.

Yield: 4 servings.

Chicken with Asparagus

2 tablespoons vegetable oil
1 clove garlic
1 pound asparagus, cut diagonally into ½-inch slices (discard tough, white portions)
4 chicken breasts, boned, skinned, cut into ¾-inch cubes
1 tablespoon dry sherry
2 tablespoons black bean sauce (optional)
1 tablespoon cornstarch in ½ cup cold chicken broth
1 teaspoon salt

Heat oil in wok or frypan; brown garlic to flavor oil.
Discard garlic.
Stir-fry asparagus 2 to 3 minutes; push aside.

Stir-fry chicken 3 to 4 minutes, until done. Return asparagus.

Combine sherry, bean sauce, cornstarch mixture, and salt.
Add to chicken and asparagus; heat until sauce thickens.

Serve at once with rice or noodles.

Yield: 4 servings.

Chicken with Rice

2 tablespoons oil
2 medium onions, diced
1 green pepper, diced
2 cups cooked rice
2 cups diced cooked chicken breast
Soy sauce to taste
Dash of ginger

Heat oil in large skillet; brown onion.
Add remaining ingredients; stir frequently while cooking over moderate heat 20 minutes.

Yield: 2 servings.

Tasty Chicken Roast

1 roasting chicken, about 5
   pounds
2 tablespoons margarine
Freshly ground black pepper
Paprika
1 garlic clove, cut into very
   fine pieces
2 onions, cut into quarters

Prepare chicken for roasting.

Dot with margarine.
Sprinkle with pepper, paprika, and garlic.

Place onions around chicken in pan.

Roast in 350°F oven until tender and nicely browned on
   top.

If desired, add potatoes or vegetables while chicken is
   roasting.
Baste chicken occasionally while roasting.

Yield: 4 to 6 servings.

Rosé Chicken

2 chicken breasts, skinned
   and boned
3 tablespoons flour
6 tablespoons corn-oil
   margarine
Rosé wine
¾ cup sliced mushrooms
2 tablespoons chopped
   parsley

Dredge chicken in flour; shake off excess.

In large skillet melt margarine over medium heat. Brown
   chicken quickly on both sides.
Pour in enough wine to cover bottom of pan.
Add mushrooms and parsley.
Simmer over medium heat 5 minutes; stir occasionally.

Place chicken on serving dish.
Pour sauce over all; serve.

Yield: 4 servings.

Turkey Hash

1 can condensed mushroom
   or asparagus soup
1 can evaporated milk
3 to 4 sliced mushrooms,
   (optional)
2 to 3 cups chopped cooked
   turkey meat
½ cup cooked peas, beans,
   corn, tomato, etc.

Empty soup into pan; heat with enough milk to make consistency of sauce.

Add mushrooms; cook gently 4 to 5 minutes.

Add turkey and vegetables.
Heat gently until completely hot.

1 tablespoon chopped herbs
   or 2 to 3 tablespoons
   grated cheese

Add herbs or cheese.

Serve hot with rice or mashed potatoes.

Yield: 4 servings.

SEAFOOD

Broiled Scallops

1½ pounds fresh or frozen scallops (defrosted)
2 tablespoons honey
2 tablespoons prepared mustard
1 teaspoon curry powder
1 teaspoon lemon juice

Rinse scallops; pat dry with paper towels.

Combine honey, mustard, curry, and lemon juice.

Place scallops on broiler pan; brush with coating.

Broil at 425°F, 4 inches from flame, 8 to 10 minutes, until lightly browned. Turn scallops; brush with remaining sauce. Broil 8 to 10 minutes longer.

Lemon slices

Garnish with lemon slices.

Yield: 6 servings.

Oyster Casserole

3 cans (8 ounces each) oysters
1 can (3½ ounces) French-fried onions
¼ cup light cream

2 tablespoons grated Parmesan cheese
2 tablespoons butter or margarine

Drain oysters thoroughly.

Spread ¾ cup onions in well-greased round baking dish, 8 × 2 inches.
Cover with oysters.
Pour cream over oysters.
Combine remaining onions and cheese; sprinkle over top.

Dot with butter.

Bake in 450°F oven, 8 to 10 minutes, until lightly browned.

Yield: 6 servings.

Maryland Crab Cakes

1 pound crab meat
6 double saltines, crushed
1 teaspoon dry mustard
1 egg
¼ cup mayonnaise
Salt and pepper to taste
Dash of pimientos (optional) chopped fine

Mix ingredients together.

Fry 15 to 20 minutes, until golden brown.

Yield: 7 or 8 crab cakes.

Crab with Red-Wine Mayonnaise

Lobster can be served in same way.

1 pound fresh, canned, or frozen crab meat	Arrange crab meat in shallow oval dish.
1 tablespoon oil	Heat oil in skillet.
1 small onion, peeled, chopped	Fry onion 2 to 3 minutes.
2 teaspoons curry powder	Add curry powder. Fry 2 minutes.
2 teaspoons tomato puree	Add tomato puree, honey, wine, and water. Bring to boiling
1 tablespoon clear honey	point.
6 tablespoons red wine	
4 tablespoons water	
Salt and pepper	Add seasoning and lemon juice. Simmer until mixture
Juice of ½ lemon	becomes thick and syrupy, then strain. Leave to cool.
1 cup mayonnaise	Stir this dressing into mayonnaise, spoon over crab.
½ red or green pepper, cut into strips	Arrange strips of pepper in lattice pattern over top; put olive into each square and slices of tomato around edge.
Black olives	Chill.
2 to 3 tomatoes	
	Serve with crisp lettuce.
Lettuce	Yield: 5 or 6 servings.

Crab Casserole

1 pound blue-crab meat, pasteurized	Remove any shell or cartilage from crab meat.
1 can (15 ounces) artichoke hearts, drained	Cut artichoke hearts in half; place in well-greased, shallow 1½-quart casserole.
1 can (4 ounces) sliced mushrooms, drained	Cover with mushrooms and crab meat.
2 tablespoons butter or margarine	Melt butter.
2½ tablespoons flour	Blend in flour and seasonings. Add cream gradually; cook
½ teaspoon salt	until thick, stirring constantly.
Dash cayenne pepper	
1 cup half-and-half cream	
2 tablespoons sherry	Stir in sherry.
	Pour sauce over crab meat.
2 tablespoons cereal crumbs	Combine crumbs and cheese. Sprinkle over sauce. Sprinkle
1 tablespoon grated Parmesan cheese	with paprika.
Paprika	Bake in 450°F oven 12 to 15 minutes or until bubbly.
	Yield: 6 servings.

Crab Meat Entrée

½ cup vinegar
6 tablespoons melted butter
1 tablespoon chopped chives
2 teaspoons Worcestershire
  sauce
1 pound fresh lump crab
  meat

Heat vinegar, butter, chives, and Worcestershire sauce in medium skillet.

Add crab meat; simmer until hot, stirring gently to blend flavors.

Yield: 4 to 6 servings.

Fish in Creole Sauce

1 medium onion, chopped
½ cup chopped celery
1 tablespoon butter or
  margarine
1 8-ounce can tomato sauce
½ teaspoon salt
½ teaspoon curry powder
Dash of freshly ground black
  pepper
1 cup chopped green pepper
2 pounds frozen fish fillets
  of your choice

Sauté onion and celery in butter in large skillet.

Add rest of ingredients except fish. Simmer mixture while you cut fish blocks in thirds, giving you 6 pieces. Put fish blocks in skillet side by side. Do not pile on each other. Bring to boil; reduce to simmer.

Cook about 15 minutes, until fish flakes easily.

Yield: 4 to 6 servings.

Rockfish Deluxe

2 cups frozen chopped
  onion
¼ cup melted fat or oil

Cook onion in fat in 10-inch frypan until tender.

2 pounds skinless rockfish
  (or other fish) fillets, fresh
  or frozen (thawed)
1½ teaspoons salt
¼ teaspoon pepper
2 tomatoes, sliced
1 lemon, sliced
1 large bay leaf
¼ cup water
1 teaspoon sugar
1 teaspoon cider vinegar

While onion is cooking, cut fillets crosswise into strips about ½ inch wide. Arrange fish over onion.

Sprinkle with salt and pepper.

Cover fish with tomatoes and lemon.
Add bay leaf.

Combine water, sugar, and vinegar. Pour over fish mixture.

Cover; simmer 10 to 15 minutes, until fish flake easily when tested with fork.

French bread

Serve with French bread.

Yield: 6 servings.

Baked Salmon

1 large can red or pink salmon	Remove bones and skin from salmon.
½ teaspoon salt	Place one layer of salmon in well-greased baking dish.
⅛ teaspoon pepper	Sprinkle with salt and pepper.
½ cup bread crumbs	Add layer of bread crumbs.
2 tablespoons butter	Dot with butter.
2 cups milk	Repeat until fish is used up, with crumbs on top.
	Heat milk; pour into baking dish at sides without disturbing crumbs on top.
	Bake salmon at 375°F 40 minutes.
	Yield: 6 servings.

Shrimp and Green-Bean Casserole

3 cans (4-½ or 5 ounces each) shrimp	Drain shrimp; rinse with cold water.
1 package (9 ounces) frozen French-style green beans	Cook beans according to directions on package; omit salt. Drain thoroughly.
	Place beans in well-greased, shallow 1½-quart casserole.
	Cover with shrimp.
1 can (10½ ounces) condensed cream of celery soup	Combine soup, parsley, lemon juice, onion, and lemon rind. Pour over shrimp.
2 tablespoons chopped parsley	
1 teaspoon lemon juice	
1 teaspoon grated onion	
½ teaspoon grated lemon rind	
½ cup grated cheese	Top with cheese.
Paprika	Sprinkle with paprika.
	Bake in 350°F oven 20 to 25 minutes, until cheese melts and is lightly browned.
	Yield: 6 servings.

Sesame Shrimp

½ cup sesame seeds, toasted	Place sesame seeds in ungreased skillet over low heat; stir until browned. Set aside.
1 pound shrimp, cleaned	Sprinkle shrimp lightly with salt and pepper.
Salt	
Freshly ground black pepper	
6 tablespoons melted butter	Dip in melted butter.
	Roll in toasted sesame seeds. Skewer shrimp.
	Grill approximately 8 minutes over grill or hibachi, turning frequently to brown evenly.
	Yield: 2 to 3 servings.

Preheat oven to 350°F.

6 tablespoons olive oil
2 cloves garlic, crushed
2 to 2½ pounds firm fish
(rock bass, flounder,
snapper, etc.)
12 mussels, well scrubbed
½ pound shelled shrimps
Salt and pepper
½ cup finely chopped
parsley

Heat oil and garlic in casserole.

Put fish in first, then mussels and shrimps.

Add salt and pepper; sprinkle with parsley.

Cover tightly with foil. Put lid on casserole; it should be well fitting.

Cook about 30 minutes, until fish is tender and mussels have opened. Baste from time to time with juices.

Serve in hot deep dishes.

Yield: 6 or 7 servings.

Bouillabaisse

Shrimp with Bean Sprouts

Shrimp with Bean Sprouts

1 green pepper (or red, ripe pepper), cut into ¼-inch strips
1 cup bean sprouts
1 teaspoon grated ginger
2 tablespoons vegetable oil
6 ounces cooked shrimp

1 tablespoon dry sherry
2 teaspoons soy sauce
Salt

Combine pepper, bean sprouts, and ginger. Heat oil in wok or skillet; stir-fry vegetables about 2 minutes. Push aside.

Add shrimp; stir-fry until heated.
Combine shrimp and vegetables.
Add sherry and soy sauce.

Salt to taste.

Serve hot with Crispy Fried Noodles.

Yield: 4 servings.

Crispy Fried Noodles

12 ounces fine egg noodles

2 cups vegetable oil for frying

Cook noodles in boiling, salted water according to package directions. Drain; rinse thoroughly in cold water. Dry on paper towels.

Fry handfuls of noodles in oil at 375°F, turning frequently, about 5 minutes. Drain on paper towels.

Yield: 4 servings.

Fish Broil

2 pounds skinless catfish fillets or other fish fillets, fresh or frozen (thawed)
¼ cup garlic French dressing
3 tablespoons soy sauce
¾ teaspoon ground ginger

Lime slices

Place fillets in single layer, skin-side-down, on bake-and-serve platter, 16 × 10-inches.

Combine French dressing, soy sauce, and ginger. Pour sauce over fillets; let stand 10 minutes.

Broil about 4 inches from heat 10 to 15 minutes, until fillets flake easily when tested with fork. Baste once during broiling with sauce in pan.

Garnish with lime slices.

Yield: 6 servings.

Fish Dinner

Fish Dinner

2 cups canned tomatoes, drained (1-pound can)

Put tomatoes and butter into medium skillet; bring to boil.

2 tablespoons butter or margarine

1½ cups diced celery
2 medium onions, sliced

Add celery and onions; simmer until onions are soft, 3 to 5 minutes.

1 pound frozen fish fillets, cut into bite-size pieces

Add fish, salt, pepper, and potatoes, stirring once.

1 teaspoon salt
¼ teaspoon black pepper
2 cups canned potatoes, drained, sliced

Cover skillet; simmer 10 minutes.

Parsley for garnish

Garnish with parsley; serve.

Yield: 4 servings.

Baked Halibut

2 pounds (¾-inch thick)
  halibut or other firm
  steaks or fillets, fresh or
  frozen (thawed)
2 tablespoons dry onion
  soup mix
1 cup dairy sour cream
1 cup fine dry bread crumbs
2 tablespoons grated
  Parmesan cheese
1 tablespoon chopped
  parsley
¼ teaspoon paprika
¼ cup melted fat or oil

Dry fish well. Cut into 6 portions.

Combine soup mix and sour cream.

In separate bowl mix bread crumbs, cheese, parsley, and paprika.

Dip fish in sour cream mixture; roll in bread-crumb mixture. Place in single layer on well-greased shallow baking pan. Pour fat over fish.

Bake in 500°F oven 10 to 12 minutes, until fish flakes easily when tested with fork.

Note: Seasoned Italian bread crumbs can be used in place of bread-crumb-cheese mixture.

Yield: 6 servings.

Broiled Fish Fillets or Steaks

2 pounds fish fillets or
  steaks, fresh or frozen
  (thawed)
2 tablespoons melted fat or oil
2 tablespoons lemon juice
1 teaspoon salt
½ teaspoon paprika
Dash of pepper

Cut fish into 6 portions. Place in single layer, skin-side-down, on well-greased baking pan, 15 × 10 × 1 inches.

Combine remaining ingredients; mix well. Pour sauce over fish.

Broil about 4 inches from heat 10 to 15 minutes, until fish flake easily when tested with fork. Baste with sauce in pan once during broiling.

Yield: 6 servings.

Italian-Style Fish

12 frozen fried fish portions
  (2½ to 3 ounces each)
1 can (8 ounces) spaghetti
  sauce with mushrooms
1 teaspoon oregano
1 package (4 ounces)
  shredded mozzarella
  cheese

Place frozen fish portions in single layer on baking pan, 15 × 10 × 1 inches.

Combine sauce and oregano. Spoon sauce on each portion. Sprinkle with cheese.

Bake in 500°F oven, 10 to 15 minutes, until fish is hot and cheese melts.

Yield: 6 servings.

Fried Fish Fillets or Steaks

2 pounds fish fillets or
  steaks, fresh or frozen
  (thawed)

Cut fish into 6 portions.

¼ cup milk
1 egg, beaten
1 teaspoon salt
Dash of pepper

Combine milk, egg, salt, and pepper.

1½ cups dry bread, cereal,
  or cracker crumbs
Fat for frying

Dip fish in milk; roll in crumbs. Place in single layer in fry basket.

Fry in deep fat at 350°F 3 to 5 minutes until fish are brown and flake easily when tested with fork. Drain on absorbent paper.

Yield: 6 servings.

Salmon-Corn Dinner

1 can (1 pound) pink salmon

Drain salmon; save liquid. Flake salmon.

1½ cups elbow macaroni

Cook macaroni in 10-inch frypan as directed on package. Drain well.

1 can (1 pound) cream-style
  corn
½ cup chopped onion
1 can (8 ounces) peas,
  drained

Add corn, onion, peas, and salmon liquid to macaroni; mix. Cover; simmer about 5 minutes.
Fold in salmon; heat.

2 slices process American
  cheese, cut in half
  diagonally

Arrange cheese on top; allow to soften.

Yield: 4 servings.

Flounder in Orange Sauce

1 teaspoon salt
Dash of pepper
2 tablespoons orange juice
1 teaspoon grated orange
  rind
2 tablespoons vegetable oil

Combine salt, pepper, orange juice, orange rind, and vegetable oil.

1½ pounds flounder fillets,
  cut into 6 serving pieces
⅛ teaspoon nutmeg

Place fish in oiled shallow pan; pour sauce on fish. Sprinkle with nutmeg.

Bake in preheated 350°F oven 20 to 30 minutes.

Yield: 6 servings.

VEGETABLES

Lemony Asparagus Parmesan

1 pound fresh asparagus or 2
    boxes frozen, (cooked)
2 tablespoons butter
½ cup mayonnaise
¼ teaspoon salt
⅛ teaspoon white pepper
⅛ teaspoon dry mustard
Juice of ½ large lemon
½ cup bread crumbs
⅓ cup grated Parmesan
    cheese

Place cooked asparagus in shallow greased casserole in
    single layer.
Melt butter; heat until golden brown.
Blend in mayonnaise, seasonings, and lemon juice. Pour
    over asparagus.

Sprinkle with bread crumbs and cheese.

Bake at 375°F, 15 minutes, until browned
Can be prepared in advance and reheated.
Yield: 4 to 6 servings.

Tangy Broccoli

1 pound fresh broccoli (or
    1 10-ounce package
    frozen broccoli, thawed)
1 tablespoon vegetable oil
¼ teaspoon dry mustard
½ teaspoon salt
⅛ teaspoon pepper
3 tablespoons water
½ teaspoon dillseed

Trim fresh broccoli. Wash; do not dry.

In saucepan with tight-fitting cover, mix all ingredients.
Cover; cook over medium heat about 15 minutes, until
    tender.
If frozen broccoli is used, separate stalks with fork during
    first few minutes of cooking.
Shake pan occasionally to prevent sticking; cook until just
    tender.

Yield: 3 to 4 servings.

Okra and Tomatoes

1 small onion, chopped
2 tablespoons fat or oil

1 package (10 ounces) frozen
    okra
1 can (16 ounces) tomatoes
½ teaspoon salt
¼ teaspoon pepper

Cook onion in fat in saucepan over moderate heat until
    lightly browned.

Add remaining ingredients; cook until okra is tender and
    mixture thickens, 10 to 15 minutes. Stir occasionally to
    prevent sticking.

Yield: 6 servings.

Carrot Casserole

Preheat oven to 350°F.

3 cups cooked carrots, sliced
1 10½-ounce can condensed
   cream of celery soup
1 cup shredded processed
   cheddar cheese (4 ounces)
¼ cup fine, dry bread
   crumbs
1 tablespoon melted butter
   or margarine

Mix carrots, soup, and cheese in baking dish.

Mix breadcrumbs and butter; sprinkle on top carrot mixture.

Bake about 20 minutes, until crumbs brown.

Yield: 6 servings.

Cabbage in a Hurry

1 medium-size cabbage

Wash, core, and chop cabbage.

4 tablespoons butter or
   margarine
¼ cup water
1 teaspoon salt
Dash of pepper

Melt butter in large skillet. Gradually add cabbage. Turn with long fork to coat cabbage with butter.
Add water, salt, and pepper.

Cover skillet; cook over medium heat about 5 minutes; stir once or twice.
Add extra salt and pepper if desired.

Yield: 4 to 6 servings.

Sweet-Spicy Beets

2 tablespoons soft butter or
   margarine
1 tablespoon honey
2 tablespoons prepared
   mustard
1 tablespoon
   Worcestershire sauce
¼ teaspoon paprika
16-ounce can sliced beets,
   drained

In 3- or 4-cup casserole stir together all ingredients except beets.

Add beets. Cover tightly.

Bake in preheated 350°F oven 10 minutes. Stir well.
Continue baking, tightly covered, until very hot, about 15 minutes. Sauce will be thin.

Yield: 4 servings.

Cauliflower au Gratin

2 packages (10 ounces each) frozen cauliflower
1 can (10½ ounces) condensed cheddar-cheese soup
2 tablespoons fine dry bread crumbs
1 teaspoon melted butter or margarine

Cook frozen cauliflower according to package directions. Drain cauliflower; place in greased 1-quart casserole.

Pour undiluted soup over cauliflower.

Mix crumbs with fat; sprinkle over top.

Bake at 350°F 20 to 30 minutes, until sauce bubbles and crumbs brown.

Note: Two pounds fresh cauliflower, separated into small florets and cooked until tender, can be used instead of frozen cauliflower.

Yield: 6 servings.

Spinach au Gratin
Use 2 packages (10 ounces each) frozen chopped spinach. Crumble 6 slices crisp fried bacon over mixture before topping with crumb mixture.

Potato Patties

2 cups seasoned mashed potatoes
1 egg or 2 egg yolks, slightly beaten
1 tablespoon finely-chopped onion
1 tablespoon chopped green pepper
2 tablespoons fat or oil

Combine all ingredients except fat; mix well. Shape into 6 patties.

Brown well in hot fat, about 4 minutes on each side.

Yield: 6 patties.

Note: Leftover mashed potatoes or instant mashed potatoes, prepared according to package directions, can be used in this recipe.

Hurry-Curry Onions

3 cups small peeled onions
1 package chicken or mushroom soup mix
2 cups water
Curry powder to taste

Cook onions with soup mix and water 20 to 30 minutes, until tender.

Season with curry powder.

Yield: 4 servings.

Sweet-and-Sour Yams and Pineapple

1 20-ounce can sliced
  pineapple;
1 tablespoon cornstarch
¼ teaspoon salt

3 tablespoons fresh lemon
  juice
2 (1-pound) cans yams,
  drained

Oil
4 scallions, sliced
1 small green pepper, cut
  into small chunks
½ cup diagonally-sliced
  celery

Drain pineapple; reserve syrup.

In saucepan, combine reserved syrup, cornstarch, and salt;
  blend well. Bring to boil over medium heat.
Cook until thickened; stir constantly.
Stir in lemon juice.

Arrange pineapple and yams in casserole; pour sauce over
  mixture.
Bake, covered, in 350°F oven about 30 minutes, until hot.
In small amount of oil in skillet, sauté scallions, pepper
  chunks, and celery until just tender but still crisp.
Stir carefully into yam mixture.

Serve immediately.

Yield: 8 servings.

Sweet-and-Sour Yams and Pineapple

Japanese Corn on the Cob

4 husked ears of corn
Boiling water
Pinch of sugar
Soy sauce

Japanese Corn on the Cob

Plunge corn into boiling water; add pinch of sugar.
Boil 10 to 15 minutes.

Serve corn hot; brush with soy sauce instead of butter.

Corn can be grilled instead of boiled.

Yield: 4 servings.

Fresh Green Beans with Cherry Tomatoes

Use only fresh vegetables when preparing this dish.

1 pound fresh green beans
1¼ teaspoons salt

Wash beans; remove tips. Cut into 1-inch pieces.
Place in saucepan with 1 inch boiling water and 1
   teaspoon salt.
Cook 5 minutes; cover. Cook over medium heat 10 to 15
   minutes, just until crisp-tender. Drain, if necessary.

3 tablespoons butter
½ teaspoon sugar
Pinch of freshly ground
   pepper
1½ tablespoons chopped
   fresh parsley
8 cherry tomatoes, halved

Add butter, sugar, pepper, remaining salt, and parsley; toss
   lightly until butter is melted and beans coated.

Place in serving bowl; garnish
with tomato halves.

Yield: About 6 servings.

Fresh Green Beans with Cherry Tomatoes

Spinach Casserole

2 pounds spinach
1 tablespoon olive oil
1 clove garlic, minced

Thoroughly wash spinach; drain.
Heat oil in large Dutch oven or saucepan.
Add garlic; cook 1 minute.
Add spinach; cover. Steam 3 minutes.
Season with salt, pepper, and nutmeg.

½ teaspoon salt
⅛ teaspoon pepper
⅛ teaspoon ground nutmeg
4 eggs
¼ cup heavy cream
Butter to grease dish

In small bowl beat eggs and cream until well blended.
Stir in spinach.
Grease ovenproof dish with butter; spoon in spinach
   mixture.

2 tablespoons dried bread
   crumbs (packaged)
1 tablespoon butter

Sprinkle with bread crumbs.
Dot with butter. Place in preheated 425°F oven.

Spinach Casserole

Bake about 15 minutes, until
lightly browned.

Yield: 6 to 8 servings.

Squash Casserole

2 cups mashed acorn squash
¼ cup soft butter
3 tablespoons honey
Grated rind of ½ lemon
¼ teaspoon salt

Stir together all ingredients.
Turn into buttered 3-cup casserole.

Bake in preheated 325°F oven until thoroughly hot, about 30 minutes.

Yield: 6 servings.

Broiled Tomatoes

3 large or 6 small ripe tomatoes

Salt and pepper as desired
2 teaspoons butter or margarine
2 tablespoons fine dry bread crumbs

Wash tomatoes; cut off stem ends. Cut large tomatoes in 1-inch slices; cut small tomatoes in half crosswise.
Place cut-side-up on broiler rack.
Sprinkle with salt and pepper.

Dot each slice with butter; sprinkle with bread crumbs.

Broil until tomatoes are soft and crumbs lightly browned, 5 to 7 minutes.

Yield: 6 servings.

Minted Lima Beans

1 10-ounce package frozen lima beans
¼ cup chopped onion
1 clove garlic, crushed
2 tablespoons margarine
1 cup canned tomatoes
½ teaspoon dried mint leaves

Cook frozen lima beans according to directions on package. Drain; set aside.
In medium skillet sauté onion and garlic in margarine until tender.
Stir in lima beans, tomatoes, and mint leaves.
Heat through until piping hot; serve.

Yield: 4 servings.

Corn and Cheese Pie

Preheat oven to 375°F.
Combine cottage cheese, Parmesan, and drained corn.

1 cup cottage cheese
½ cup grated Parmesan cheese
1 can (12 ounces) corn
Salt and pepper
¼ teaspoon paprika
1 canned pimiento, chopped
1 cup cooked peas
1 8-inch baked pie shell
2 tomatoes, peeled, sliced

Season with salt, pepper, and paprika.

Add pimiento and peas. If mixture is a little stiff, add some liquor drained from corn.
Pour into pie shell; arrange tomatoes around edge.

Bake about 15 minutes.
Yield: 4 or 5 servings.

SAUCES

Sour-Cream Sauce

1 cup sour cream
1 tablespoon chopped fresh
  or frozen chives or
  green onion tops
¼ teaspoon salt
3 drops Worcestershire
  sauce
White pepper, as desired

Combine all ingredients thoroughly at least 2 hours before
  serving. Refrigerate.

Serve at room temperature or slightly chilled.

Can be served with broccoli or baked potatoes.

Yield: About 1 cup.

Cream Vegetable Sauce

1 can (10½ ounces)
  condensed cream of
  vegetable, celery,
  or mushroom soup
½ cup half-and-half or table
  cream

Combine ingredients; heat.

Serve over vegetables, meats, or fish.

Yield: About 2 cups.

White Sauce

1 tablespoon
  polyunsaturated
  margarine
1 tablespoon flour
1 cup skim milk

Melt margarine in small saucepan; remove from heat.

Add flour, stirring with wire whisk.
Add milk gradually; return to heat.
Stir mixture constantly until sauce has thickened.

Salt and pepper to taste

Season with salt and pepper.

Yield: Approximately 1 cup.

DESSERTS

Peanut Butter Crisps

Preheat oven to 350°F.

½ cup flour
¼ teaspoon baking soda

Sift flour and baking soda twice.

¼ cup (½ stick) butter or
    margarine
1 tablespoon white sugar
¼ cup brown sugar
½ teaspoon vanilla extract
¼ cup peanut butter

Cream butter, white and brown sugar, vanilla, and peanut butter until quite soft and creamy.

1 egg

Beat in egg; stir in flour; mix well. Put on unbuttered baking pans by teapoons about 1 inch apart.

Bake 10 to 12 minutes.
Remove to cooling trays.

Yield: 24 crisps.

Peppermint Chocolate Cookies

Preheat oven to 400°F.

1 cup flour
1 teaspoon baking powder
¼ teaspoon salt

Sift flour, baking powder, and salt together.

½ cup shortening
½ cup sugar

Cream shortening; add sugar; beat until light and fluffy.

1 square baking chocolate
A few drops oil of
    peppermint or ⅛
    teaspoon peppermint
    extract

Add melted chocolate and peppermint flavoring.

1 egg, beaten

Add beaten egg.
Add flour alternately with milk.
Mix well. Drop by teaspoons onto ungreased baking sheet.

Pecans or blanched almonds

Flatten with knife dipped in cold water; place pecan or blanched almond in center.

Bake 8 to 10 minutes.

Yield: about 25 cookies.

Peach Melba

1 package (10 ounces) frozen
  raspberries

½ cup currant jelly
1½ teaspoons cornstarch
1 tablespoon cold water

2 cups cut peaches
1 quart vanilla ice cream

Place raspberries in 1½-quart saucepan; allow to thaw.
  Reserve a few whole berries for garnish. Mash rest of
  berries with spoon.
Add jelly; bring to boil over low heat.
Dissolve cornstarch in cold water; add to raspberry
  mixture.
Cook until clear, stirring constantly. Strain; chill.
Place peaches in sherbert dishes; top with ice cream and
  chilled syrup.
Garnish with reserved whole berries.

Yield: 6 to 8 servings.

Ice Cream Pecan Balls

1½ cups pecans

1 quart ice cream

Hot fudge sauce

Toast pecans by spreading in shallow pan and baking at
  300°F 15 to 20 minutes or until lightly browned. Cool;
  chop.
Shape ice cream into 6 balls. Roll balls in pecans. Place on
  tray covered with waxed paper; return to freezer until
  firm.

Just before serving, top balls with hot fudge sauce.

Yield: 6 balls.

Ice Cream Sandwiches

1 quart ice cream
12 graham crackers (plain,
  cinnamon-flavored,
  or chocolate-coated)

Slice ice cream into 6 slices; place each slice between 2
  crackers.
Serve immediately or return to freezer until time to serve.

Yield: 6 sandwiches.

Ice Cream Snowballs

1 quart ice cream
½ cup flaked coconut

Shape ice cream into 6 balls; roll in coconut.
Place on tray covered with waxed paper; return to freezer
  until firm.

Yield: 6 snowballs.

Jiffy Pudding

1 package (4 ounces) instant
  vanilla pudding
1 cup dairy sour cream
1¼ cups milk
½ teaspoon vanilla extract
½ cup chopped, toasted
  almonds

Combine first 4 ingredients; beat 1 minute.
Add almonds.
Pour into serving dishes; chill.

Yield: 4 to 6 servings.

Pears à la Ritz

Fresh Bartlett pears, halved
Vanilla ice cream
Hot fudge sauce

Place half a Bartlett pear in shallow dessert dish.
Fill hollow with vanilla ice cream.
Top with hot fudge sauce.

Yield: As desired.

Strawberries Romanoff

2 pints strawberries

½ pint vanilla ice cream
1 cup whipped cream or
　whipped topping
Juice of ½ lemon
3 tablespoons orange liqueur
　(optional)

Wash, hull, and chill berries.

Soften ice cream slightly; whip until fluffy.
Fold in whipped cream and lemon juice.
Add liqueur to berries, then fold ⅔ of berries into cream
　mixture.
Spoon into parfait glasses or brandy snifters.
Decorate with remaining strawberries.

Yield: 6 servings.

Crazy Chocolate Cake

3 cups flour
2 cups sugar
2 teaspoons baking soda
⅓ cup cocoa
1 teaspoon salt
½ cup salad oil
2 cups water
2 teaspoons vanilla
2 teaspoons vinegar

Mix dry ingredients in 13 × 9 × 2-inch pan that will be
　used to bake cake.
Pour oil, water, vanilla, and vinegar over dry ingredients;
　stir with fork until mixed.

Bake at 350°F, 30 to 40 minutes, until cake springs back
　when lightly touched near center.

Yield: 13 × 9-inch cake.

Boston Cream Pie

1 9-inch yellow cake layer
　(made from cake mix) or
　1 package (15½ ounces)
　chocolate-chip snack
　cake mix
1 package (3¾ ounces)
　instant vanilla pudding
　and pie filling mix
1½ cups milk or light cream
3 tablespoons cocoa
¾ cup confectioners' sugar
2 tablespoons hot water
1 tablespoon butter,
　softened

Prepare and bake cake according to package directions.
　Cool cake completely.

Prepare vanilla pudding according to package directions,
　using only 1½ cups milk. Chill until set.
Cut cake into 2 thin layers. Spread filling onto 1 cake
　layer; top with remaining layer.
In small bowl, combine remaining ingredients until smooth.
　Pour glaze onto top of cake; allow some to drizzle down
　sides. Chill until ready to serve.

Yield: 9-inch layer cake.

Lemon Pie

1 unbaked 9-inch pastry
   shell
1½ cups sugar
2 tablespoons flour
1 tablespoon cornmeal
¼ teaspoon salt
3 eggs
⅓ cup milk
¼ cup butter or margarine,
   melted
¼ cup lemon juice
2 tablespoons grated lemon
   rind

Preheat oven to 375°F.
Mix sugar, flour, cornmeal, and salt in large bowl.

Add eggs, milk, butter, lemon juice, and rind. Beat with
   rotary beater or electric mixer.

Pour into pastry shell.

Bake about 35 minutes, until filling is set and top is golden
   brown.

Yield: 9-inch pie.

Come-Again Cake

4 cups all-purpose flour
¼ teaspoon salt
2 teaspoons baking powder
2 teaspoons mixed spice
1 cup lightly packed
   brown sugar
2 cups mixed dried fruits
   (currants, raisins, etc.)
¾ cup soft shortening
2 to 3 eggs
Milk

Preheat oven to 355°F.
Grease and line loaf pan, about 9 × 5 × 3 inches.
Sift flour, salt, baking powder, and spice together into
   bowl.

Add sugar, fruits, shortening, and beaten eggs; heat until
   all ingredients are well blended.
Add milk as required to make soft, dropping consistency.
Put into prepared loaf pan; smooth top.

Bake 1 to 1¼ hours. Let cool a little in pan.
Turn out on cooling rack.

Yield: 9 × 5-inch cake.

Fresh-Fruit Upside-Down Cake

¾ cup butter or margarine,
   room temperature
1½ cups firmly packed dark
   brown sugar
2 cups cored, pared, thinly
   sliced fresh apples or
   pears

1 package (18.5 ounces)
   spice cake mix

In small bowl blend together butter and brown sugar.
   Spread mixture on bottom of two 9-inch layer cake pans
   or one 13 × 9 × 2-inch pan.

Arrange apple or pear slices over mixture.
Prepare cake mix according to package directions; pour
   into pans.

Follow baking instructions on package.
Cool cakes in pan on wire rack 5 minutes.
Invert on flat plate.

Yield: 9-inch layer cake or 13 × 9-inch cake.

Fried Bananas

Fried Bananas

¼ cup flour
1 teaspoon cinnamon
6 bananas, sliced lengthwise

2 or more tablespoons
   shortening
Sugar

Mix flour and cinnamon together; thoroughly coat each
   piece of banana with mixture. If bananas are very long,
   you may prefer to quarter them.

Heat shortening in medium skillet.

Brown floured bananas slowly, turning once.
Remove bananas to heated platter; sprinkle with sugar.

Yield: 4 to 6 servings.

Chocolate-Marshmallow Pie

Chocolate-Marshmallow Pie

2 squares (2 ounces)
   unsweetened chocolate
2 tablespoons sugar
½ cup milk
12 marshmallows
1½ cups whipping cream
1 8-inch baked pastry pie
   shell
½ cup chopped toasted
   almonds

Put chocolate, sugar, milk, and marshmallows into top of
   double boiler; stir over hot water until melted. Let cool,
   stirring frequently.

Whip cream; fold into mixture.
Pour into pastry shell; sprinkle with almonds.

Chill thoroughly before serving.

Yield: 8-inch pie.

Cherry-Berry Cake

Cherry-Berry Cake

½ cup margarine
¾ cup sugar

Cream margarine and sugar.

1 egg, beaten
⅓ cup milk

Add egg; mix well.
Blend in milk.

2 cups all-purpose flour
2 teaspoons baking powder
½ teaspoon salt

Combine dry ingredients. Add to margarine mixture.

1 No. 2 can cherry pie filling

Spread half of batter into greased 8-inch-round container; cover with ¾ can pie filling. Spread with remaining batter; top with remaining filling.

Bake cake in 375°F oven 30 minutes or until done.

Yield: 8 servings.

Chocolate Cherry Bars

It is advisable to make these the day before they are served.
Preheat oven to 375 × F.

8 squares dark baking chocolate

Break chocolate into pieces; melt in double boiler. While chocolate is melting, grease well an oblong shallow pan, about 11 × 7 inches.
When chocolate is ready, spread over base of pan. Put into refrigerator; leave until set.

2 eggs
½ cup sugar
1 cup finely shredded coconut
½ cup candied cherries

Beat eggs and sugar together until light and frothy.
Carefully fold in coconut and cherries cut into quarters.
Spread mixture over chocolate.
Bake about 15 minutes until top is firm to touch.
Remove from oven, let cool.
Refrigerate overnight.
Cut into bars, remove from pan.

Confectioners' sugar

Sprinkle with confectioners' sugar, or sandwich two bars together with chocolate inside.
Yield: 24 bars.

INDEX

63